abecedarium

THE UNIVERSITY OF ALBERTA PRESS

dennis cooley

Published by

The University of Alberta Press
Ring House 2
Edmonton, Alberta, Canada T6G 2E1
www.uap.ualberta.ca

LIBRARY AND ARCHIVES CANADA CATALOGUING IN PUBLICATION

Cooley, Dennis, 1944-, author.
    Abecedarium / Dennis Cooley.

(Robert Kroetsch series)
Poems.
Issued in print and electronic formats.
ISBN 978-0-88864-645-3 (pbk.).— ISBN 978-0-88864-827-3 (pdf)

    I. Title. II. Series: Robert Kroetsch series

PS8555.O575A24 2014   C811'.54   C2013-908393-6
                            C2013-908394-4

First edition, first printing, 2014.
Printed and bound in Canada by Houghton Boston Printers, Saskatoon, Saskatchewan.
Copyediting and proofreading by Peter Midgley.

A volume in the Robert Kroetsch series.

The University of Alberta Press is committed to protecting our natural environment. As part of our efforts, this book is printed on Enviro Paper: it contains 100% post-consumer recycled fibres and is acid- and chlorine-free.

The University of Alberta Press gratefully acknowledges the support received for its publishing program from The Canada Council for the Arts. The University of Alberta Press also gratefully acknowledges the financial support of the Government of Canada through the Canada Book Fund (CBF) and the Government of Alberta through the Alberta Multimedia Development Fund (AMDF) for its publishing activities.

for douglas barbour

And just as there are pleasures in the rhythmic passage of air through larynx and over the palate to be beaten by the tongue and pressed against the teeth, so there are the parallel pleasures of pressing pen into soft paper, the stylus into clay, of hitting the keyboard of a responsive typewriter, or watching the lines of letters appear in the glow of a monitor. Memory serves us well through this material and returns embodied as the witness to our having made certain moments into a record on the page while the temporal life of writing aches towards the future, longing for that recovery which is available, again and again, through the physical form inscribed with information in the trace of material.

—JOHANNA DRUCKER, *Figuring the Word*, 74–5

No object is in a constant relationship with pleasure.... For the writer, however, this object exists: it is not the language, it is the mother tongue. The writer is someone who plays with his mother's body.... in order to glorify it, to embellish it, or in order to dismember it, to take it to the limit of what can be known about the body: I would go so far as to take bliss in a disfiguration of the language, and opinion will strenuously object, since it opposes "disfiguring nature."

—ROLAND BARTHES, *The Pleasure of the Text*, 37

contents

PREFACE

this she said
this is what
you need
to know
if you want
to write

/in english

- there are 5 vowels to indicate 50 sounds
- there are many descenders, y among them, ours is not to reason y
  the alphabet is very close to the ancient greek and roman in
  sequence and in lettering
- there are many ascenders too though as senders no nor ass enders
  they wont amount to much [some would say they are endless and
  should stay at home]
- some readers object to typographic impertinence, get in a terrible
  guffuffle, a nasty snit
- the nineteenth century let loose a barrage of new fonts that shouted
  for attention, at least when the merchants got hold of them they did
- riddles and gnomic utterances since ancient times impeded naked
  communication
- a young Toronto poet is an avowed and out-an-out lipogrammatist,
  unrepentant some have said from too much book learning, gives us
  too much lip

- it is a wonder that in writing R so much can be done with a bowl, a vertical stem, and a leg stroke. Perhaps, ~~dear poet~~, dear reader, you might find this information informing, if not provocative. Prof Ligate, for one, might.
- some readers say typefaces proliferate to express different meanings
- the first books were designed to resemble manuscripts
- readers can make out almost any variation on a letter; this is especially true in dealing with pharmacists and editors, also doctors who as failed calligraphers are richly rewarded
- runes were scratched on wood or bone. Odin found them, wrote the first poem. A big guy from Gimli did the same, up from the ruins.
- words in early manuscripts were often fused continuously and were hard to extract in the reading and so to make out with any distinction
- punctuation as we know it was settled only after printing was well established
- same goes for spelling
- attempts to develop a phonetic alphabet have been frequent and often have ended in disaster
- ghoti, writes George Bernard Shaw, spells fish: gh from enough, o from women, ti from nation
- ghoughphtheightteeau spells potato, someone else has shown
- the double U was a double U
- Wynkyn de Worde printed many books in English vernacular
- spelling was anchored by print and the sounds of words floated further and further away from the letters. Cast adrift, they sailed out of sight, and once they did people began to talk a different tune, began to sing a different song—sea chanties behind their backs chansons reels flings dirges chants ballads graffiti swearing contests the purchasing of coffee the pulling of toffee and silent letters. which often as not they left, began to complain of spelling & wrongful pronunciation. a sailor in every port. acts of piracy, unlawful seizure.

at the window

at the window
glass children
circa 1951

the beginning of the word
their pink mouths
weak suns of winter
feel the chill

       open

  "**aahhh**" they say

as if in crow or ton
silitis tongue-tied

  ○○O-**O**○

pull warmth out
the small quiet
engines of their lives

  OO!°°O

press their lips close
till they touch the cold
refuse the circle

    open an oval

into which they breathed
shape of their small lives
spreads   moistly
softens the frost

abo ovo

egg so clear they can see
                        ahhhh!
    almost through
    the albumen
    the aluminum cold
    on the other side

                        later learned they had
                        blown holes in the O-zone
                        the sun could flood through
                        the bubble they lived inside
                        holding their breath
                    holding the earth's membrane
                        no longer in tact

4

a child's book
of verses

is it simply perverse to suppose

                x versus y

  what could be worse
than to begin with "**A**"
as in aleph as in ox

    in verse & re
  verse to plow one
under is to blow a kiss / is to create

            an ear
it ation in it or in re: iteration is it to raise

            an eye

     brow a fur
   row ed brow to blow
   hot & cold to turn
   the other cheek to
    turn around

          completely
  free the pro & con

   versely & which may be worse
  to be a blowhard
  would be a hard blow
    to bear

       to run

a ground set sail get carried
away find a nother
                    word a nether
region to be from
     that kind of reverberation
that running ~~aground~~ around

may also be to wobble
                from time
to time deterred im
     peded in ad
vancing in not plowing
     on straight a
              head hell bent
     or unbent
in no way averse
                    to changing
          positions having
erred averred turned
to another tune tried
     a different step

     away awry wary of
being turned
          on   down   aside   up
side down
                         steered hither
          & yon
fly to spider
                    stretched near & far
a way as well
                    you know
     damn well
you cunning old bastard

a long
funny book

I'm thinking of calling
        this a long poem.
I'm thinking of calling this
        a long funny book.
    Well it is.
It is when you compare it
        to George's. It's not
    a comic book
& it's not a cosmic book
it is a funny book.

George's was not.
               You could tell
        it was

    a short sad book.

I'm telling you George
           & it isn't
    funny. Funny he sd
           you shld
      say that.
             That's true
            that's what
            I said.

what about being
(for a change) de Sade
is fied defy the odds
the old gods & new
gods deify
damned if id
be the one & do it
be pure gold man
panning for allophones

This, this one is long
and it's funny
lots funniern George's
and longer too,
if you think for poetry it's long.

Gertie's was a long gay book
she was pretty spry & she
knew she knew
what she was doing
she knew up from down
when from where & hence from here
but from or and and from and
she knew that too
she knew or pretended
when she was
talking about
& so did George.
George will know that

                    this, this is a long
                           funny book.
                    Not a comic book
                    but a funny book
                 in a funny sort of way
                      a cosmic book
                    in its own way
                                          coloured.
A gnomic book.

                    See for yrself.
                    Don't take my word
                    for it you go
                    ahead read that
                    book George wrote.
                    He knows his isn't
                    it isn't funny.

I'm telling you & it isn't
not one little bit
& that is why
                           he said
        it was sad.

It was kinda sad all right.
When all is sad & dun.
It is sad, or so it has been said.
Or shld have been.
George himself should have

"LET IT BE
SAD" HE SD
"DON'T LET IT BE
SAID" IT IS NOT
AS HE SD.
AND SO IT WAS
SAD. TOO BAD
IT 'S SO SAD.

                  & so
that made him.

                                     sad it shld have
                made him sadder.
          it shld have made him madder
          it shld have made us gladder
He shld have made it
                even shorter.

                                    this story is
                                  said but new

          but you knew that

sammy b
makes it
to estevan

a haven to some
a kind of heaven

is that so
so is that
that's it
is it that
it is
that is it
is it that then
it is
that that
that it is
that is so
so that's it
that's it
all right
it is so
that it is that
it is

                                        it that is
                                        so it is
                                      that that is
                                      so is that
                                     not this that
                                      that that
                                    so that is that
                                        that's it
                                   so that that is that
                                        so it is
                                     that that is so
                                   but not this that
                                   no that this is not
                                    so not this that
                                    this not is that
                                    then this then
                                    so that is that
                                        that's that
                                      is that it
                                        that's it
                                        that's that
                                    tkk tkkt tthht

          is that so
           so it is
           so is it
           it is so
           so is it
        that is where
            it's at
        that it should
        come to that

                                                   so it
                                                   goes

in the book
of secret
alphabets

the alphabets of the seven planets
the alphabets of the twelve constellations
these being the celestial alphabets

the seven alphabets of the learned men
the four and twenty alphabets of other learned men

the antedeluvian, no more than three in number,
of which the first Adam spoke

and in which he wrote his books
the tree alphabet
the Oriental alphabets
the seven most celebrated old alphabets
there is also the runic alphabet

in which were forces to help in love
and illness, fertility, and weather
and countless others in whose letters the world is enclosed

all these and more being the books of nature
in which the secrets are written
in which knowledge is hidden
in these scripts the wisdom of the ages are written

the alphabets speak to those who might know
record what is and what is related

speak to those who know how to read and cipher
and from those who should not hear

to keep all things secret
no less in acrostics and anagrams

in irony and paradox in metonymy and synechdoche
that the letters not yield meaning or purpose

that they conceal it from the uncaring and the inattentive
that none unravel its knottings unless pure of art

that none undeserving says the poet should find it
                            in any way
a musing or make the least
            sense of it

OF SUSPECT WORDS FROM THE FILE: tammy:

a

affections

an

are

begin

blue

buys

cold

dark

each

entanglements

example

as

also

and

by

begins

both

causes

colouring

distant

early

entering

eyes

actions

altogether

apparently

be

believes

but

clear

connect

distinctly

encouraged

evidently

for

fervour	fiery	fulfill
gaining	her	he
hair	have	here
his	him	horse
how	is	implications
important	in	it
knows	luck	may
man	might	money
more	moreover	mother
need	needs	not
of	on	out
overtones	paragraph	paul
please	possibility	possesses
powers	pubescence	recognize
reinforces	relationship	remarkably
resemble	restructure	rides
rocking	satisfy	second
sentence	sentences	set
sets	sexual	sexuality
should	signify	stage
such	surprise	taking
tammy	tap	the
that	theme	therefore
those	to	topic
tries	trying	us
up	very	verge
wants	we	what
when	with	woman
you	your	yours

the means justify

always said didn't i
say the means
just if I the and
if i just hadn't said
and that's not all
mark my words
it's all anyone can do
to make ands meet
this way or that way
to make am ands
any way that's why i am
ands to your buts a
men to that that's what
i say it all ends up
at the and and
to com pound matters
to make matters worse
it is at hand
it's all over huh
and that's not all not by a long shot

under the h is the and
        this sordid little sore T
we have put a damper on
        an ampers and
that's not all there is sand
        under foot and we want an and
to it once & for all
        we want it fini
shed shut down kaput finis
      we want a stop put to the in
        fini tude you've got to and it to us

          you have reached   a dead and
           you are a dead   ringer for
            there is no   finish to this
             none what   so ever

      wheresoever howsoever
        you would swerve
      this sorry story its so poor
      ly furnished the world be
hind us now is bad
    ly served
so sadly finished
        alas we watch our B
        hinds collapse sing before
        the swinging balls
of Irving's ump ire
that bias that alias
what have we done to deserve
this and in addition what's more
a change in empire

                                              but not until
                                               it all goes
                                         in every thing goes

                    in so far as it goes
                    as far as that goes
         we all forego
           do not
          fore close
           its not
          far to go
                   for so it goes
                                        on & on

to the next line
              the next time
                      to be so well
                                        coordinated so equal
                                         in measure so fine
                                         in timing & in time
                                        i will be putting you on
                   hold why dont you just
                   hold there jest a minnit
                   now jes hol yr horses

     you could just close the book
                    its up to you
           go a head   you've shut me
              up on this one
           you can do me in   all right
              do me in in the and
           you will get your chance

& if it
changes

& if it changes
from SOV → SVO
& its pre

positi on flips to post
posit ion what does
that do

to the act
i on to the pro
position is it lost
in trans it

ion what then
of the cop
ula what about acce
pella is that

accept able or is alle
gory what of purga
tory tory tory
catch a tory by the tale

what then becomes
of singing or of signing

]the bureau
crats the aggl
lutin ate a plant
i grade run wild

the same of shame
ful creates & crates
of painful syntax
create an impasse
the sham bling & elon
gated got so me
one who wants to

im press o bf us cate glued to
the self for emost & hindm
ost a tan gle of pre & suf
fixes mad spilling of la
tin poly pro genit

ive said it is as
i have told it
to you as you
here have he
ard & read
there it is then
wha t's so hard a
bout that

hyoid

Allowing for the creating of a great reach of sounds that other
creatures cannot make, it enables many movements in tongue,
pharynx and larynx by holding them beside one another to
produce remarkable variations.

    it being neither of Ovid nor ovoid
    how then to speak of it or avoid
    hybrid if only in rhyming
                  in loving
    the sound of the words
    in our mouths to howl
    & so to release the moon
    from the darkness in our throats

                what when in lack of
           we being avid and wishing
             to speak are devoid of

                        what then in long-legged time
                         to make of the high bird
                             crying in the elms

where the bone being disarticulate
    brings into art
iculation breaks voices from our necks
shooes them onto the hot dry air

why this shy bone that lies
hidden at the back & shoves
       & how is it   ·
suspended by muscle & ligament

      what slip page do we risk then
         bidden to speech
      in wet & cartilagenous zones

            "shaped like the letter up silon" (*u*)
            with up so floating many sounds
            round as an initial
            letter it was a rough breathing
            & from which in rome four more
            letters arose: V and Y and
            much later U and W

all those forked & hollow letters
the small hoe hooked in
the tongue weeding the noises

            also a small horse
          shoe of hope & wish
         that hoards its sounds
         within its shape stashes them

         small dish of phonemes
         which when we're dead
         and hied out of hiding
         falls silently out of our heads

& what then of the four
obsolete letters we know
as Dig amma Qoppa San
and Sam pi late of
lately deceased
come at last to O
mega or to Zed which
ever comes last
so abso
lutely

love non-alpha

love non-alpha
)numeric style

       INSERT:

    backspace
    control
    delete
    end
    enter
    escape
    home
    return
    shift
    space
       tab
          key
                  &
                      then the the the
       last thing you would have imagined the
             spatter of am
                    persands
perhaps
             in hopes of
     spitting on everyone
  's feet

many persons loathe & fear

        the some old am

per sands are running

    or not per se

out on them or out-and-out

    running off

not to mention around

    their amp

er age at their age more than ample

    on a saturn

day night or alia this is

    getting us there

        & now faces

a sudden failing a falling

    off all amplitudes gone

    all that is platitudinous what ever is

    multitudinous & they feel as if they were

    tied up in nots

    all would be for naught

    whatever études or attitudes

but in the end the ands are

    always true

to you and your con

    junctions your in

    sistence on

    coupling with

out the slightest comp or supreme

unction without a thought for proper pun

ctuation & spell

ling & us wondering how

it could possibly function or you thinking

it should be fun

ctioning shunnning in such terrible com

posure or position or portment

who can be sure under such incompletion

the word has not fallen into depletion

you can't beat that can you

bet on that its be at i

tude it casts

its own kind of letters

creates quite an attitude you got

the ampers

sands speck

ling the page almost unfettered trick

ling through & through

it's tough trying to figure

or follow through

such nonsense

a sidewalk rain splots

the smell of dust & wet when

it hits

& the page breathes

easy again equal to

the down fall the water

spout our hearts are

bruised go pop

soda opening

or brussel

sprouts in fall

c'mon and get over it

c'mon and get over it
and and it over id say
this is a stick-up
etc. etc.

&

it would be awfully sweet
my sweet old
in the and
and in and in and
you & me wishing
we would be there
til the very and of rhyme

lewdly acting loudly
hoping in the and
you me we
would have it
fully we believed we did we
had it cummings

& that above all
it would never and
never in a million ears

oh look look
look & see
see jane spot
see dick jump

this is an eye
hook with which
eve took my

breath &

away you took me
take me oh peggy
dear to your heart
& clutch me too
near to your & bosom
we two to play

a little &

you win
some lass you lose some
the & sum total
ity of our mort- & mor-
ality in all reality
in & raging be
as tiality
to tally un
ending in spend
thrift days & short

shrift nights shiftless hours

un class   if id it in

forming & it lined with glass

  our lives shining

     bottles glmmering

  with & baubles

            &

    &

deixis

deixis: e.g. in

I came yes
terd ay the refer
ence of I will be to who
ever is spea king on some
specific occasion to
day perhaps and then the time re
ference of *yester*

day will be to the day
be fore the one on
which s/he is
doing so a
matter of w)here
and w(hen one is

fully regis
tered undeterred
when you saw which
way the words were bl
owing and from whence they came
trailing loud with st orrie

hence you were then
what you say then
              you are

ready to begin :

                    that'll be the day

so to speak

i.

                         other than stammer

              uhh **uuhnh**

     UuhhHnn

                   UUGHNNNN

hard ache to speak   the continuous   motion   pushes
                 pushes pushes   ushesushes   ushers

freely one moment spoken   language for ward in more or less
knowing for a second regular waves, as the muscu lature of speech
its nature min gling in or gans tighten and re lax in
                       slippery tissue puls ates
before speech each to each through the trough of words
at which we drink though where also & thereof we speak
                      past sinus cavities plunge
          and hear yearning each
     for each more or less

                    other wise hardly to be borne
                  the affliction in words
                 hard pressed to resist
             mute to multitudinous
          mountains of words impugned

                your immunity weakened by
-passed over if you insist
                if you must
    on the lee side the other
side where you do not feel
the chill of ice and snow
                    beside your self
over selves with whatever breath
    pulled out of bodies
        hankies from sleeves
                        sadsweet magic of our lives

its catch in the throat & throwing
        he is going to record
        the sounds of women
        in many languages
        when they call out
        in orgasm how would they
        differ what would they say
tricked by the virus spiralling
  into your ear trick-
                les like a carra
                    way seed
        or spider that's been

    carried away what you
being cosmopolite being hayseed
most feared words like a the

saurus spreading on rock & honking &
                        always & long
have dreamt at midnight we might
come down with such an infection
the smallest inflection felt
copula that couples us together

ii.

for this is a game to be so
    way laid led astray as
          strays do & go
good as lost as
    trays may
        spill or
  gasm gasp
        leap the gap

        on frog year leap hope
          yr ear alert
        conduit to the heart
          waiting to hear
              & take it in
          the warm spit & sound
        shiver of that in the ear

iii.

earache ear drops tear drops
quick as arachne as sharp
a lover a moving & lou
vering woman or man
ouvering up & down scales
practising by the hour hoping
to plunk the guitar strings to the heart
trinkle keys to affection in G
      -Major B-flat
lave all dry and wakeful thoughts
leave them far behind their veering
    oh little boy blue
blow from a fat horn
      corn you copia
  the ow's in the warm

iv.

        spoke in such over
-tones & -tures such note
-worthy sounds yes s/he said seeing
herhis doubt hihers double
     go ahead s/he said
       in a wetting of lips

          take it
one of them both of them said
             it's yours
    yoursyoursyoursyoursyours
           seize the ay
       why don't you won't you you are
wont aren't you she wanted to say
   s\he hoping dear god s\he is
       at sea at C
the very seas seething
            in their ear
  rings utterly ear responsible
the voices sonorous
          rough and liquid
their bodies roaring in & out
  want to tide the tide the stem
in stamen & pistil past all
       stammer or stutter
       utterly fluent
totally re: prehensible
completely sensible
carrying on like that all summer
     all winter too

v.

in like manner
hums whistles cooings

oons oons oonnns
nNn mmmm they say
in/out in/out taking &
sending sending & taking
they are oceans crashing
gorges filling
HHHH GHHHNNN
sounds of inter mingling
the throaty as piration we know as desire
& sometimes love

vi.

uhh unhh

uhh hhuhh
unh huh
unhuh
uhn
uh

vii.
if only you
would lie down be
side beside myself
beside yourself
with joy

The seven scruples of Kroetsch

(being also known as the seven principles in sleight of hand):

1. Palm—To hold an object in an apparently empty hand.
2. Ditch—To secretly dispose of an unneeded object.
3. Steal—To secretly obtain a needed object.
4. Load—To secretly move an object to where it is needed.
5. Simulation—To give the impression that something has happened that has not.
6. Misdirection—To lead attention away from a secret move.
7. Switch—To secretly exchange one object for another.

—adapted from *Wikipedia*:
http://en.wikipedia.org/wiki/Sleight_of_hand

where in
the ear

st while re:
ader swirls an adder
                side wind
er twists & so on

        finds him with out
        friends among fiends

                you writers
                that's all
                you see

                for you
                every thing
                is black
                & white is
                    n't it

you know
what gets me

no. what?

that.

that's what gets me

that's what gets his goat

that's how s\he got me

that's where it gets you

that's who really gets me

that's when it really gets to me

that's where it gets tricky

that's why it really gets you in trouble

what?

/that

that's what she said

not that it matters but

that's what you need to know

that's what

what?

that

what that?

this that

that that?

why not that this?
yes this that
not that that

oh that's what
i thought it is
this that then
when it's you
speaking that is
that that for me
what's that to me
that's what i want to know

yes that's what
i've been trying
to tell you
when this that
is or is not
your that this
is where we can un
ders tand one
an other

what's that you said
what's that got to do
with you and me

it's a simple matter
of deictics of picking
up (on) a few pointers
following the old tip
isn't it you and me

it's you or me
and this or that
this and that
and the other things

       nearly every time and every
       place what could be
       clearer what more direct
       what now & then more perfect

               what's with this
               what's with you
            what's come over you
            i don't know what's
             the problem that's
              what's so funny
             yeah funny they think
           this is hard that's what
            they say that's what
             i can't figure out

       listen you've got
        to get me
        out of this
         or that
         will be
        our down
       fall this time
       same as last

     that's what
     I'm trying
     to tell you

if you know what
's good for you
if you would only listen

                                        so what
                                       what if
                                     what then
                                     what now
                                     now what

          what's that to you
          what's that you say

               pay attention why don't you
                      i told you every
                          thing i know
                          that's what

feet first

what it is to stay
afloat to keep your feet
to say on your feet in an ill
-fated and flat-
footed world to say let's call it
off if the cuff
link is not there the ear
ring does not ring
& this is not
a fate accompli
or feet accompli
shed shed call quite a feat
her life effete
let alone   all along
a life that is tarnished

shed said it was so
marvellous all of us
so fleet of foot
so quick of tongue
we rolled like marbles
in the porous cosmos claimed
it was high (she too)
ly accomplished
widely acclaimed
deeply admired

and would be so always
were we not playing
footsie was i not myself

tipsy and putting on
    heirs and was she
                    not paying
        falsely with me
and if you are you could
        you could do it
others too practically every one
            spill / tip / push
me you her them off the page over

the margin into a wilder
ness where winds strafe
  our messy hearts swim
in loch ness or swarm
            its wide crevasse

& just whose wideopen are you on
                /any way

alas fear not you say neither be for
there also is the ace of spades
the ache of maids there
            after & ever & even
                more hidden for
                    bidden to you
the queen of hearts playing
her part in greensleeves
    and day thumps
  is a pace-maker &
presses a thumb into you

so moved your heart swells full to bursting
so proved where the blood bubbles
& you explode like a beet feet-first

something to gladden the heart

badly
overt-X-ed

o what an é
criture am i what a creature
at yr service what me
to nymies i meet on my
way to the can
teens counting (on) the way their knees
are greater than mine, clearly
ease their way through

out on parole from mar
king down the gray stairs down
the square art dreams in
4 or 5 women
in stupour of hormones
loaves swollen with march
round the corner &
there she is
there

mind tilted on the banks of the slippery signifier
aporia supplement means origins traces presence
all there   before yr very nose almost

                  & then there she is her
presence her sense that always
before has left your breath
                  left you near
      ly breath
less before speech nearly when
ever she's been or not been
in her absence tracing

you have seen her before
you have dreamt her behind
she has been on your mind
        you can't get over her you
        wish she were all
        over you   above all

                  & then she is there
here she is
            then there is her
        smile in her hand out
                        for you here she
        says you have it you
            hear her
                    say st. pa
        trick's hear her
        smile louder than ire
land though she can't be irish
yet for st. patrick's day she says
go ahead it's yours she too is

            yours a green card
                        what's this
        a condom she says
        thanks you say & no
        damn wonder you

can not con

demn no nor under

stand can only dream

more deeply the ways

to the station

coming after im

-passable paths the impasse you reach

how impossible it wld be blind

spots gaps gaping the veiled words contra

dictions you hang on to the end

of desire in language:

sign above a green sham

rock "in case you get

lucky" it says shameless with fantasy

the slippery signifier is this

shamble of desire for old

langue's sake & my own too if i her

best interests had at heart or parts

in hand one thing

you are certain you are uncertainly putting

off infinite deferral unending longing

how in the end you cannot bring

yrself try though you might

cannot revel in unrevealed life

the in bet ween & all that

that entails that

in the end you might be

completely over

come come

pleatly overt

X-ed

prefer ring

- the Romans learned to add serifs, small finishing strokes, to their monumental letters, perhaps to confer grace and stability upon them, there upon THE TRAJAN COLUMN, perhaps to help stone carvers in incising them more neatly and easily, perhaps to call in law and order: look out, here comes the serif. No lower-case permitted.
- modern designers say the serif helps to clarify letters and so to aid in the easy apprehension of them, offering a wall to ward off the "halation" of light from the white paper (Firmage, 211)
- and what about the sans serif, sans souici. I'm not yr type said muse to poet so sweetly winsome
- these were the letters of Empire, the Trajan, incised in granite, and they created a sense of power and majesty
- the Nazis at first favoured black letter scrypt
- the monumental letters were very hard to write and they were so large they filled the surfaces of expensive writing material
- even worse, the lettermen got tired, sprained their wrists, contracted arthritis, broke their bones, poked their eyes out, lost fingers, it was dangerous being a letterman in rome
- Roman letters developed for inscriptions and their shapes bore the mark of the chisel but not the pen
- the stylo was used to make deft incisions in clay, to form letters by hand, you would show your hand, they could read in your hand in the half-baked texts, your hand, your very own style
- miniscules were called for, something the hand could form quickly and compactly, the loving cup

- the ancient Romans experimented with shorthand
- to punctuate is to puncture the skin the surface of, poke holes in arguments, make incisive comments
- states moved quickly to control the print trade, as had the church before them sought to control the word
- among ancient Greeks the ruling families for the longest time disdained writing as fit only for the rude and the vulgar, this before electricity came in and candles became chique, the alphabet a crude arriviste, sweaty tradesman who had not the capacity to remember and enact, offending its betters who were occupied in performance and feats of recitation
- the Vulgate made a big difference
- rhetoric was the measure of a young gentleman, the felt force of words, spoken, speak that i might know ye. L.O. Quence. Hence, which they ate with slivers of Quince.
- new typefaces appear as there is a felt need for new forms
- a language settles down when SACRED TEXTS are printed
- †HE BOOK OF KELLS is stunningly beautiful in design and execution. Through its letters flowed the light of god in jewelled and radiant colours.
- and what of glyphs? and hieroglyphs? of ligatures?
- if you recite the alphabet—26 more or less, sometimes more, sometimes less—you will have spoken all the letters of all the words that in english can ever be spoken or written, letter rip, take er to the nth, the rest is up to ~~others you~~ the entire syllabary the whole shootin' works
- in some languages you do not write vowels, do not dare write them, thx xnspxxkxblx sxxnds xf gxd
- when the material we know as Homer was eventually gathered, shaped and put on the page, Homer, who up until then had been a bard, a bird word, became an author
- the doubleyu is a gutturally-modified bilabial voiced spirant
- the same word in different typefaces is not the same word **same word** same word *same word*

- some very clever lipogrammatists drop a particular letter from entire texts. Or keep. Bok bok bok bok they say. Poultry in motion.
- it took the slaughter of 5,000 calves to provide the hides for the thirty vellum copies of Gutenberg's bible, i kid you not
- the word bible comes from an ancient city, Byblos, famous for making the papyrus used in γρεεκ books
- the majuscule and miniscule are lower-case and upper-case because of where printers kept them from frequency of use, for ease of reach. In any case what's what they say.
- in gyromancy people went round and round a circle of letters until they lost their balance and fell on letters which spelled secret messages, in domino, the power of the spirits, husha husha
- sometimes a rooster pecked grain off a circle of letters and revealed words, what there was to know, hence forth and birds of a feather, signs of things unseen
- papyrus was so expensive that Egyptians used both sides and even washed off old texts, your mother washed your mouth with soap when you used dirty words
- inspired Egyptians would wash off the letters in beer, then drink the beer so that the words would be theirs, taken in and known. some still observe this ancient practice. some brought to hidden eloquence then even take to speaking them.
- many once believed that words are given by the gods and suffused with wisdom and would in chant and recitation release their powers
- many believed letters had miraculous powers
- some say the letters come from ox and house and sun
- the Romans used wooden tablets covered with wax as surfaces upon which to write, and thus invented magic slates of the ancient world
- later there were hornbooks in the time of Shakespeare and some poets still mention them, the large- and the small-hearted still later later still

fabrication 7

knot:

        a tight cluster /of people
fastenings formed by looping and tying
together something twisted and tight and swollen
a soft lump or unevenness in a yarn either
an imperfection or created by design
to tangle or complicate
knot that you'd notice, knot that it matters
knot that you'd ever let things rip

                      tangle:

an involved account, an insolvent account
to twist together or to entwine, licorice sticks
      it takes two to tangle

                two to lick
               two to like
             two to tingle

                    ravel:

       as in run
you are always running
out of time always travelling
      i see i say you
have a run in your stocking
why do you want to run
out on me revel in such way

wardness reveal more fickle-
than naked- ness
is it nice to rave about this
you and your socks appeal
so to entangle so to disengage

tease:

to raise the nap of
to raise from a nap
to disentangle and raise the fibres of
to annoy someone playfully or maliciously
a ribbing, a ribbon of provocations, a string of prevarications
occasions previous or present some ribald most not
someone given to teasing as in mocking or stirring up
a seductive woman who plays with you
in offer and withdrawal

cotton:

to take a liking to

wool:

to pull it over
her eyes and there
you have it the eyes have it yes they do
there in the scratchy darkness
touching on dreams of linen & cashmere
to bring near
hold dear
to feel itchy

material:

things needed for doing or making something
an artifact made by weaving, felting, knitting, or crocheting
fibres concerned with wordly and therefore bodily interests

having got her hook into me, that's what matters is
directly relevant to the matter, crucial to the issue
having substance and weight not in
any way imaginary or made up
what i say you say is immaterial to you
though it is the real thing here & now
what goes into that is
what makes things up

                                    felt:

i never felt like this   /never
detected by instinct or inference
as when a sensed presence in a room raises
goose bumps on her arm

                                    pin:

a number you choose and use to gain access
axis consisting of a short shaft that supports something that turns
cylindrical tumblers consisting of two parts that are held
in place by springs; when they are aligned
with a key the bolt can be thrown that is this is
a consummation devoutly to be wished.
flagpole used to mark the position of the hole on a golf green
a holder attached to the gunwale of a boat that holds
the oar in place and acts as a fulcrum
                              for rowing
                  to hold fast
what is found in a haystack or on a wall   /
what some put on the wall id be embarrassed
you cannot pin this one on me
                        pin the tail on
            the don key hohtie
tall tale if ever there was one

hallelujah

aeua

aleua

aleuja

haleuja

haleluja

halelujah

hallelujah

hallelujahhallelujahhallelujahhallelujahhallelujahhallelujah
hallelujahhallelujahhallelujahhallelujahhallelujahhallelujah

hallelujah

halelujah

haleluja

haleuja

aleuja

aleua

aeua

aeua

    aeua

        aeua

                aeu

            aeua

      aeua

        aeua

it is
significant

surely so much so
how can we be saussure
that in these chance collusions
confusions of speaking
darned if id defy her
deify perhaps dear god yes
dehumidify perhaps
that this word and that word
would in the damaged world
meet might speak could squawk

it is an old sense of letters is it not
(stout or long) an arn old
ian sense through eons
that vowels might in season
blow like the owl in open throat call
out through the long consonants
stiff in rectitude certain in their identity

like the owl in open throat call out
through the long consonants
make music in their passage

speak songs wish memory
in their moving down & over
giving tissue to the skeleton
in the breath of the world assembling
the sounds of matter life mending
the music of their motion
across through the stiff frames of language
the five senses stirring
the five vowels finding

                              /the stops\

sediments settling inside
the ear im balance
the world in collusion
colloidal with cold
alveolar with grief

meaning

meaning

me
an
ing
me and
you ing
me and
er ing
erring per
haps the ear
rings awry

or else
me an
de ring
right it is
a mean
ing i mean
me and er
or ring
me and her
her o to ing
to her o i bring
oi oi
i o

i o
her
a lot
o i
i like her
a lot
but that
that's an

other thing
as i wish her
to sing
every sing
le temps
as i mean to say
as we say
to mean
: meaning

a me
ah me a
mea
culpa
a culp
rit /right
writ large
having writ
ten times ten
i told her
a hun
dred times
if i told her
once the then

ten thin lines
that's all
it's all
a matter of ten
shun of a cipher
ing
etc. &   &

i ask you
then
                then
is every
thing gone
as kew s/he said
i ask you
just becoz

you was me
we were there
we two you & me
were here
there we were
there you were
& there was i

who was i
who were you
who are we
to say
i was me
a ning
a ming
a mong

we had
run a muck

the things
that matter
i mean
i meant
to say

i plan
to bring it
up i hope to
bring you around

olito's
suknaski

sez that's you it's you suknaski:

        he's got me
unscrolls the pages of my life & stretches
the paper rubs until the hair falls
dark & curly as a sheep

oh andy who made thee
only my head though he touches
does not filiate into anything

     i say
       it's me /suknaski

it is vellum there are veins and stains from time
pitted into if you wish you could write upon
stipple of blood calligraphy of skin
        the sun has tattooed
     i say but no one listens

think these are old stories written
       on and in my skull glistens
my mouth opens air rolls up and out
i become a character in a comic book

if you look out you can see
them slippery and floating
fish out of the nets my thoughts lifting
head off the corner for all i know the colour of light bent
its membrane sliding to the bottom of memory

the frame watches you there in a chair reading
lines i once dragged behind ripping open
furrows in the prairie searching
for sounds a crow scrolling
the torched air

will when they find me here say
i am ginsberg i am a rabbi
rabbit or coyote they cannot tell
rabid perhaps when they look they can
and can not yet see

a bearded man a child's face
eyes that turn back turn black at the glass

thrown back on my face a darkness
passes across the oat fields that
blow in my mind

good pitching
is almost
always

a matter of shatte

RING bats & ex

pectations

that is ill

egal in its fli ght & in its re

lease less than

but a strategy off ol lowing

fast pitch es with sl°w in

side wit ho uts ide on

ly the Knucklebal l hOw

ever sets up X pectat ions co

nfouNds

the mrene ws the m a nd

bet rays the

m in theco urse

o fa sin gle

pit c

H

it ^{fl} _{o-a} ^{ts}

flu^{uu}_uu**T!**te

r S

tWi **t**_{cH}^{e.s}

luR

CHES

an

dd i_{ve}

s

or so it seems
a pro perl yhuRled **Kn**u CK _{le}
balls ee Ms toma Ke
u pits owN (mIn d
on th

eW ay

u p

to t hE P(P(P(P PP
: late

it's all in
the seams
in the seeming to be
:108 stitches in red
waxed threads that join
two pieces of cow
hide to form the cover

the effect of spin is potent a slow .
roll even if just
a few

                degrees per se
cond
                        gives
          the k)nuc
k

                                leb al,l
            its moti
       on

—adapted from James Gleick, *New York Times Service*

a slip of
the pen

is to be

come he puns bene

fitting from a slip

a mere slip of

the pen

is it to be

trusted

in

to be N

trusted it is only

fitting slips

up seeps

in

ink false

leads it lays

nebulae upon night

sky inverted con

verted to a new

script sure

the photograph we know is
sun-writing there in cinema

you can smell the
sin
in popcorn &
feelings

up smearing light pen
celling daubs
walls smears ceiling

& writing then yes
you have heard is negative

you know all about
michaels
flies

black lies
the comma

toes of spiders fly

specks that struggle
to rise from pa

per they stick on

& mon kish

we bend over

the whole world now

deeply non de
script

kitsh & maw

kish   /sheesh

One big fat zero

one big fat zero

    an O
oh a zeer?
you mean a zeer- oh!
        oh!
no: an oh
    O! an O?
yes that O
        it is not
known nor is it oh
so full of zeros is it
    to the last syll
able of time babble of rhyme
nor though you may wish
& believe will ease it her or you
      is it a bra
-zeer in which we find
two of them
      (two) (Os)
           (O)(O)

as you must
    have no
           tissed
ttssk tskk
tho yr daze
           is numb
    ered & erred
   hardly 'eard in her O
-zone you can see
the score: zilch
bugger all nada
    it's because of the no
    ise isn't it

   ask No
one but NO
        AH
ah yes Noah
Noah knows then
with him it's No
Ah or No One

perhaps a No Go
No One Nose
    will do OK
for in these matters
one's nose is out of joint

that's it it's him
the old no it all
the nay-sayer?
ever yea-slayer

yes: him.
N.O. then?
NOH An O
Anno Domini of Our
Lord watch my lips
oh what lips these
these lips in ellipses
for in craft adept
in cleft adroit
on stage performed
what could ever eclipse
who would ever know
what is left out or
in nil or null
annulling & so
o mitted also ill
or well fitted

this surely must please
    oh no no
no? what no? why not?

who nos where the wind
goes?
whose slips are these
whose two lips
whose slip-up
        or down
heads you lose
    tails i win
oh tulips in heaven
havin' such a time
heavin' there
having her way here
with me beside
my self by her side
seeing her this way
    & that way
wetting her lips
letting on to be in
  terested oh
a longing OOOOOO
    no not O
not so youd know
at least an E long
gated in elan
       to be O
penned you can
(or cannot) depend
  on that
    / that O
  on that note
an O to be noted pro
moted above all others

two Os to be doted upon
a zone to be crossed & wary of
desirously to be sought
hoping she will owe you big
                ooo oo
            she sighed
XOXOXOXOXOX
        she signed delighted
    to have been in
    -cluded -vited -spired
        to be utterly in
    decent to have been
    so vitiated & so
    among eyes to be dotted
                one of the star
        crossed lovers
    who were it not
            for the kluges
    we could scarcely tell apart
    when they appear together
        swollen or squeezed
    looking more & more appealing
    one of the Os that has been
                my oh my oh my
    wheezing like an accordion
    in some body's hands looking
                    i know
        to say is appalling
    swollen or squeezed out or in
                    to shape

for her for him
it was touch & go
it was tick-tack-toe
it was playing footsie
it was keeping time
        or making it
all the way
home again
riggedyjig

and so on & so

forth to quest
ion on go forth to

start at the out
set the on set
the setting out
the setting on
the putting out
& putting on
a putting forth
a sallying into
the setting

sun I hence
my self
forth to be
a hero not one
on err ands
act ually to be
her o o to
venture fourth
when yr worth
a lot more than
an o her one
& only o
her very own
in the odd ad

                    venture
                   meant yr
                  wrong it is
              wrong you are it is

                          time to be on
                          to be on time
                          O mega time
                          making big time
                          for the time
            being to babble
         on that or an alpha
          & to be come beta
           particles of faith
          you can bet on that
         A men to that that re
          petition & so on &

           so & so
                 it goes
                        on & on
    it goes & no body knows
         where it stops
              & so one goes

                          forth &
                     foregoes it all adds
                       up in the and
                     if there is no and
                    in sight you can keep it
                            up & coming see
                      where it gets you

loade your crafte with

           ors and buts

know when the or is exhausted

believe there is
   a divinity
shapes our ands

Bill is a bloomin' loomin' airy

One of the Discworld's most implacable gods, and very difficult to understand. He looks like a pleasant, middle-aged man, but his eyes are starry voids. It is possible (although difficult) to bargain with him, but proverbially impossible to cheat him, although this has been done at least once. (When Cohen the Barbarian rolled a 7 on a six-sided die by cleaving it in half in midair.) He is known to play games against The Lady using mortals as pawns, and always plays to win. His Temple is a small, heavy, leaden sanctuary, where hollow-eyed and gaunt worshippers meet on dark nights for predestined and fairly pointless rites. He is said to come from a world other than the Disc.

and Bill has given
The Word that shall be
to all peep
ill Bill has shown
The Way
on account

of Bill has saved a lot
of money he has gotten
ten or a lot more from many
pee pall when they went/
dig it ally when they dipped
into the glowing
MS font

//

O Bill King Billy has heard
hysterical men & women say unless
something drastic is done & so he has
o pened and shut
the gates in our heads he has shouted
his 10 commandments his terror of
error & core ruption
10 10 10 10 10 IO IO IO IO 10 10
IO IO it's off to Word I go IO IO IO
he has said as he moo ned the world
& i thot he did beli eve
it was an open & shut
case the late st
decalogue of yeas & nays
)beats Keats
a lot of people say some nay-sayers the billy
acres thot
he owed us
big he thot
he owned us
nothing owned us

out right we were so decadent
no 2 ways about it
in an arch deaconal move

Mr. BiG had bought us fair and square
 and brought us to
 stood us up at

 the glowing windows   where as one
of the Holy Mess angers we might
gaze and in glowing faces & growing witness
 as at the inn or manger
 and the very best excel
 he would take us
make us on the spread
sheets pay for our sins

all we had to do was get right
down on our knees
 & pray
 things would work
 now the Word was out

 Bill has shown us
 the door
 way to DOS fun
 da mentalism
 the talis man
 the fund amen
 ts of life
 we speak tskk tskk tskk he says
we are part of His Entourage
 & we are free or not
 no need
 fear not Bill's Word

for in his world he can cure
ailing ligatures can work such changes
　　　　with the mere laying
　on of ands he has written
a new scripture that we might
day & night write in a new script
or ium and there will be a few small
　　　　service charges the odd bill

DOS sayeth Chairman Bill
　　in riddle & cryptic
LO I am IO and I in blind light
ning strike　　fear into
and many felt a thrill run over
　　and some a chill
knowing he would be with us all ways

　　　　　　　it says over and over again
　　　　　　　if we do not all will be lost
　　　　　　　　　Bill tells us fear
　　　　　　　　　　not my people
　　　　　　　　for i can bank on that
　　　　　　　　　you have my Word

　　　　　　for his is The Word
　　　Chairman Bill has promised
　　　　has given us The Word
　　　　　　　the final ill
　　　　　　uminated MS.
　　Word that shall determine
　　　　our every rumination
　　　　　　if only we would
　　　　　let Billy have a go at it

it tells on all digits
when we write
when through the shining
and coloured glass before which
we bend and read

this document
cannot be saved
before conversion
please save

on a blue screen these words flashing

**PLEASE
SAVE
PLEASE
SAVE
PLEASE
SAVE**

this is true

move this page where

ever you want why

should it be

here at

all why not take it

right out if

you think

you are better off

with out it i

only put

it in in the first place

because some times he

will say this this is true

but may be he does

not

like this and i should

not say it but it

still is true even

if he did not

say

it it is all true this

is is not it

even if it is neither

here nor there

where would we be then

crow speaks
of first & last
things

it's a skin game a thin name this alphabet of desire people writing upon
their bodies waiting on all those hearts & snakes waiting to be written
the sacred signs scared of nothing at the hinge of ink & skin hung from
ladders they shine brighter than sin a kind of velum they wear upon
their hopes their bones stretch across cross themselves scant as ants
in january can count on it it is on scriptures scraped clean & so say the
scribes as it was written luminous in letters the careful ink the cold &
hunched scriptorium god runs tirelessly the scrape & script or let me
make myself perfectly clear it is the scrap heap for you you who need
monkish devotion to the embroidery tree where crows make doilies
daily dutifully dilly dally as on heavens skin they print tattoos have
nothing to do with taboo what to do no nothing to do but hang around
tangle with the bright blue sky being resent patches in the lesson for
the day recently indecently spread on parchment they ink their way
through the merest pretext the sinking feeling there on the horizon they
may be sin kings speaking omega to have spoken first to be speaking
last at first of last things at last of first things as it was written is now in
snow & ever shall B often the second letter unto the end the last of the
roller-coaster winds when yea all those with funny names shall be last,

eh, when the thirst is come upon & the roll is called the roster named zygpelski's name is mud and crows stung by the frost of such reception all those endless attempts to foist texts upon them cry from the knotted & broken threads the threadbare weeds that they are sick & tired of tests write non descript messages of their own parachute their blotched and leaky scribblings onto the stained glass heavens letters they try to stain and strain to from and badly want to send madly think of recalling

i don't know

who or why

& i

oh i

i was

never over

you over

joyed always

meeting

you in this

ligature

OIOI OIOI OIOI

io io io io io io io io io io io io io io io

I	I	I	I	I	I
O	0	O	0	O	0
I	I	I	I	I	I
O	0	O	0	O	0
I	I	I	I	I	I
o	o	o	o	o	o
!	!	!	!	!	!

oiy yoi yoi such joy seeing you seeing

i was disappointed i think is the word

though as for that one

might say the world is seeing double

jointed loosely hinged nearly
inarticulate with what it thinks
                    it wants

        my word you say what is the word
        coming to why didn't you tell me this
        the word has gone astray goes
                this way &
                                that way
            that way i am

confused at every turn
until i don't know
  what to expect
                        which way
        to turn
    what in the word am i
supposed to do

                    when you can't spell
                    when i can't tell
                    where you're at
                    where you're going
                    what you're going to

        do or say
            i say
                i see
                i say
            i was never
                    over you
            not once
                    /ever

as for me &
my id

id take an and
/any old day
m'lady

i really wld
here on the corner of more and and st
at the corner of yet again st
id be up against it
a ghast you might say

id not and by idle
not on st and i wldnt
& let the word sidle past
derelict as an abandoned poet
\that kind of angst
no way im goin to take that
lyin down
definitely not
i am against that sort of thing
i think you should know

you understand surely
now the id is off
piddling little id tho it be
now i've blown
your cover i told you
over & over darn right i wld
id be there no que
stion right then & there
i told you
you can count on me
count me in

first thing you know there id be with the and
in sight in the and id be
prepared to face the but

if it came right down to it
in these small & par
simonio us times
o minous with self-regard though they be
mutinous though you may wish
there's always more there's always and

and so id be good and ready
to face the but
and if it finally came
to that i really wld
gladly i wld
be giddy i wld
coz there is or in themthere ills

never mind i can take it
there where run the ands of time
and it all adds up   ends up
the mountainous past the mutant & mutinous now
drinking together light from the lamps
and gladly
glad anding there in the purple glades
of ~~eternity~~   perpetuity you might say id
learn to adore the lore of

either/or
not to mention
but or and
god for
bid such unending amore, eh?

¿why would you men
shun it

there on the stage
couch of life
touché id say
better pull over & turn
over the goods

id do such things
& what is more
lots more
these things we cld abide

or lower bid for
mid able or not id be better
prepared to take
the but/and of life

it all ands up you know
all the niggling and piddling
all the loops & knots
no matter what you say
the word throws at us
those frayed thoughts that glue
like mar
malade m'lady such a terrible malady
you in all things melodious
how sad you must face these malodorous things
that such things should so upset thee

oh dear us
you & i we two
we too
to male
diction stooped
to such stupid & cupid
in ous acts heinous ways duped

all you need

do is ask

narratologee

nar
rat
olo
gee

? w
h$_y$w

he nith
ink
ofy
ou doi
thin ko
fan
M
bedded
stor
Y

how odd
she said

she wasn't all that odd she said
how old is he is she old too then
what after all are the odds

my word id just as soon call it quits
hand it on and see what it adds up to
what the word amounts to

it's an old story isn't it
the small addition of sound
the dash & curl of ink
                    /that ambition
        a diction you know
                (in an airy voice)
        or used to know ought to know
                    the small audition of their talk

was it admonition when she asked
some form of ablution some hint of absolution
                    was it such a terrible addiction
dear miss lonelyhearts what would you say

what does it matter

a few grains of sand
a few drops of water
art in part
icles of faith
the icicles in your heart
four parts laughter one part and

after we conduct daily additions every one of us
apply every morning to play
ourselves when we aren't
& when no one else is
looking of course s/he we dawdle in the door
swindle time of its talk
it's a matter of adoration in consequence of

and no one knows how or where
to stand or how
they can possibly stand it
so we all stand at the door and we stand around some more

it does not add up
ultimately we are held
in and between these tall letters pen
ultimately lined up like overweight cops
as they are written, reel by
in time we feel

the full force of the law
real as it appears in paper and pen
alty such erudition no one dares
question or requisition
face charges of slippage and repetition

their deepest wishes
their moist and secret whisperings
our 11:00 p.m. lives open and waiting
creatures with wet wings
snails at night that slide over clay
petition cold to touch
words that flip   (inside ellipses

listen they say

we say

why so upset

mums the world

listen they we you me he she wouldn't
breathe a word

of this to anyone
you hear me

so help me god
we took an oath
& they did too
the two of them

and oaths were taken
our words were taken
from us stolen & placed
in new (or old) editions
were not talking sedition here
they were solid as noah
should have been comfort
to the heathen a warm shoulder

faced with such erudition
our word ought to have been
good you would have thought it was

but

you weren't listening
were you dear
reader oh no
                not you
so pleased with
your own ear
    rings & doodles
your own making up

you, you could see
from the word get-go
their words were
barely audible

in addition they were
scarcely legible
they were not
worth the paper

they were
printed
on

they didn't amount to
much by this time terribly
addled the author added
hoping to impress

the runners press

the runners press
into snow scribe two
   lines hiss
their parabola of moving

inside the chink & jingle
 the huge horses
snort brightness onto the air

  [;p[[;p[[;p[[;p[

one black one brown drop

woodcuts onto a page
they step across

   ching *ching ching* **ching**

   at the back behind the cache
  the eggs that lie in straw a creche?
      we (my
 sisters & i hold
   an iron bracelet
 the cold sprays in our faces

                    slew out & over over & back
                            cross & recross   the tracks
                    dark pearls winding the line

the intense white inside which
we squint before & after
    fall & make angels

snow which in winter thaw will resemble
            icing on doughuts

                    reveal marks of horse and sleigh
                    runners & kids closely trail the music
                    -box inside which our father bends
                            & conducts
                    cold so intense our faces
                    burn & pinches our breath
                    until in bright scarves it rises

     my father studies the bluethin horizon
            steadies it there &
                            wipes his nose
            half-frozen snot
on the back of his fat mitts
    smacks them together against the season

                    clean as fresh laundry
                        crossing january
                    1 o'clock fields on a saturday
                    in which we are loosely bracketed

                        on the way to town
                        shakes the music
                        out of the reins

fabrication 4

I'm not threatening, just telling
and you darn well need to know
you are behaving in an unseemly fashion
your talk so thread-bare and frayed
it is a tissue of fibs and fabrications

it was evident she was up
braiding me up one side
& down the other hers was
a sharp tongue her remarks cutting
remarkably plain as it turned out
plain and simple she was prepared
to shout my lack to the world
watched like a sulky spouse for a way to take issue
take out her scissors & take it out on me

at which point he knitted his brows
feeling put upon by her deftness
                 with knives & scissors
her importunacy definitely her shear obstinacy
        and he poor knave only browsing
lines formed on his forehead when he spoke

oh yeah he said he knew not seems

                    though it suits her

             to weave such a story

her theory filled with fray & pilling

      a clear case of bias

hers was a warped and twisted view

   when it came right down to it

it was all there   right before her nose

on the very prints she was admiring

        plaid and sample

                  she could look it up

         if she dared

                darned if he would

        do it for her

home
thoughts

where does it

　　　　　　　　does it

　　break

　　　　　here

or

　　　　　　　　　　there

　　　　　　does it

　　break　　at all

the right　places

where or when

　　　　　　　　　　might you make

　　a break for it

　　　　— a mad dash to freedom

why don't you

　　　　　　give me a break

has it never occurred

to you that i

　　　　　　　might need a break

might want to take a breather

　　　　　　　　　　does it ever

break up　　　　　　　　　or fall

                    a part
        of a new line
                            made a new
                make a new
            now   how does it act
up on you
                        does it leave you
    breathless does it
            bring you gasping
to the breathing hole

                till death doth us part
            & you you are pretty
            broken up about it be
            cause breaking up is hard
                    to do   is it
            not dear reader

what would you say

÷

what would you say

++A+ +⊙U++ +⊙U +A+ i+ i +Ai+

i +⊙+E +⊙U

+EA+i++ ⊙U+ A++ ++E +⊙++⊙+A+++

would you hear me still
red-eyed desperado on edge
riding across the dusty page
rounding up vowel inside consonant
utterly inconstant soundly inconsistent
where they mill & drool

where i myself having heard
though i look silly i suppose
call & whistle at every stray

WH+T W++LD Y++ S+Y +F + S++D

                              Y+P   /+TS TR++

+ L+V+ Y++

               L++V+NG ++T +LL TH+ V+W+LS

would that make any difference
you in your barbwire horse
-on-fire affections bawling

could i make myself any clearer

wht wld y sy f sd

                              yp tstr

lvy lvng t ll th vwls

÷

would you see me whirling over
head a long & loopy syntax
    dopey grin inside the snaking

watch me awwshucks making
            consorts of a brandnew alphabet
COWBOY X making my mark in SIDDLER'S GULCH
cattle performing operas on the open range

would you believe me when i make
            consorts of alphabet
    runaways & stayathomes i have rounded
            up where they wandered
                    all over the page
    converts of letters there
            id be coated in dust
barely able to breathe the name of god

oh poem poem on the orange
sun oh give me a hint where the cow-pinchers squint

    tis a sage & holy thing i do
                  in the rustled air
        reading the sundial
          the residing light
              dust shines on
await the growly weather as it rowells
across a hot & gritty world whips at my heels
two small suns spinning

the whole world law
        less sans

             serif holding
its hands & watching
anxious with uncials
             unctuous too
              if need be
              is what i
                'd be
known & wanted

            ÷

what could you say

till someone was able to come across
a barren land down with a sinus headache
that or a droopy moustache

  it is a scandal
      it really was

what would you say

wht wld y ſy f   ſd yp tſ tr
lvy lvng ll th vwlſ

leaving out all the consonants

/those growls

leaving out all the vowels

/all the ahs & ohs
abjectly unadjectivally unadverbially
leaving everything up in the air

would you feel badly shaken
would that matter
to you would you too
feel left out & trying to read
between the letters
where X marks the spot ✇

how could you

put an end to such brand
new be ginnings

what would you say if i
right out loud
up & said

yup   /strue

i love you

÷

oh im leaving it
leaving it all

up to you
my dear
reader scanning
the horizon

+n th+ +nd
+ts +p t+ y++

s+ch + p+t+
y++ d+ n+t r+pl+

what would you say
if i said

i love you

putting in all the consonants

putting in all the vowels

leaving it all
behind leaving it
all up to you

dear muse

dear muse what's the use
pretending we know where this is
going to end or why i am your out
landish & dashing figure in your o pera
& you yourself limbs akimbo O
lympic in movement limber
emotions thick & sloppy as soup
muddy alembic to your thoughts
your modus operandi shady as a water tower

why it is i should have to be playing opus
sum tell how i came to be your one
                             & only
    all yours all limbs

              iamb iamb iamb
no lamb no nor goat though as nimble
& in desire as great surely believe me
i am the iamb come to the laughter
    I M I M I M I M IM
  mabi i am mabi mabi
may be i am May Bee im not
  may be this is my B
             & it may be im not

i dont know
why you say

why you say i dont know
know i say why you dont
i know you dont say why
why say you know i dont
i say why you dont know
why know dont i say you
dont know why you say i
you know why i say dont
say why i dont know you

i dont know why you say
say i dont know why you
dont know why you say i
know why you say i dont
why you say i dont know
you say i dont know why
why i dont say you know
why dont you say i know
why dont you say i dont know

Pref:

- the wearing of phylacteries and amulets shows a belief in the power of letters
- abecedaries are organized on an acrophonic basis, in alliterative ordering
- handwritten letters vary enormously. some poet's signings are so notoriously illegible readers find the very inscription they want.
- writing was opposed by bards and scholars because it was the work of crass upstarts who knew nothing of true knowledge and grace, had no memory and hence no real appreciation of things which they should have learned by heart
- if in Rome you were ostracized the verdict would be taken by writing names on scraps of pottery called ostraca
- the sound of the letter N has changed little over thousands of years
- because there are so many right-handed people the practice of writing from left to right took hold, so that scribes would not smudge their writing as it snailed in a wake behind them
- the Greeks had seven vowels and Apollo on his seven-stringed lyre played the music of the universe
- the Hebrew vowels were never written, nor the phoenician
- the vowels some believed were the expression of the soul and the breathing of god
- harold innis, like plato, feared that the new literacy would lead people away from considered thought and public concern
- plato feared the language in the body, prayed for its death, the revolting vibrations in the flesh, loathed orality

- innis feared that monopolies in the new technologies would obliterate local life, tempt us to the fake ill of innis free
- some believed the vowels expressed human emotion and the consonants acted to modify or to constrain them, wind blowing into a tent, the canvas tugging here and there. pegged in constancy. the word a well into which vowels would flow, filling
- I am the Alpha and the Big O, the big end, sd The Big Man. O Mega. No micron.

lungs
flapping

(for douglas barbour)

the air up

the throat an elevator

brain an incinerator

headed for light

you feel light

-headed when it

drags itself up

& over

epi glot tis roof tongue cheek teeth lip

clouds scrap ing rain off

the mount ains a roundness

threads into pock ets its into

clicks that go off like tickers

into murmu rings and buzz es
air that cre ates dings and bur stings
exp losions of lips vib rations
in bone a gul ping off lesh

a ru shing through
bone ands oft tissue
tis of you & of us
ho ldings to pa late
a cur ling of tongue
a tigh tening of ch
eeks the pres
sing to tee th
a to ngue ins ide
we tness moving
war mandt hick

> birds e scaping
> thew armth of their f light
> the moistness the most
> ness of their lives

in the green or
chards of our talk
the silk clouds are burning
the ir music

every *w* here ri sing
rin sing
us out

at any and

i myself will

or will not

oh no will not

lift a finger though i will

have a finger in the pie

yes of course rest assured of that

i may even burn my fingers

if i don't keep them

crossed or out of

the way this way

i will not let up

let us per

severe or con

versely since this is

a set up perhaps

even a set back

it could be a stick up

you got to sit up

& take notice

it's enuff to

though to tell the truth

ive had it

with you i got

to hand it to you

with you i will keep my hand
in i swear you or i
will have y)our hands full
if you in turn take things
in hand or too far put your hand to

let me put it to you
this way it has come nigh
& it is at hand lo i say unto you
          come hell or high

water things may exchange hands
              this living from
        hand to mouth
           from time to time
              now & then living
     mouth to hand too
man this is really living

mouth to mouth is not to be
sneezed nor should anyone down
one's nose look nor turn one's nose
          for of such is
the kingdom of havin' if such
          should happen
              we will up & pull it

off handed & down unless of course
     word gets out
                    things get out
     you know
more than you might imagine
          out of hand & turn

into run a ways & we may
have to throw our hands
in or up you yourself might say
how many times do you have to say
hands off though admit it
how ever off hand your words
you find me aw fully handy
have said more than once
you have found my hand & me
my self more than a little hand
some & then some when
your having forced my hand
        hand over hand i climb

        to your call haul my
self up the walls of your suspicions
through halls you have lined with derision
dragged all the way to your nunnish cell fearing you

might take my head off or my hand
thinking you will take it & run with it
                /planning to make a run for it
                        pretending it is a hand

-off imagine you when you take the ball and run
with it heading off in all directions
though i think you should
refrain you really should just because
you were you say dealt a bad hand
dealt a serious & life-altering blow

what about me and my painful brow-beating
you've still got to play your hand
that's why we should shake

hands & other parts i think
you should slough off
your dereliction you should show
your hand & every one
of your other 218 parts
as soon & as often

as possible under the circum
       stances i would luv
heading off for parts unknown
you pretending you don't
like it putting on
quite the show

type face

did not want to
do an about-face
stand shame-faced
in full frontal
put on a **bold face**
the effrontery of

thought of
prínted letters
matter set in type

qualities common to a number
that distinguish them as
characters by which **R**
elations hip be
tween though **E**
lusive may be
the form common to
ALL IN
stances of a ty pical
and often super

ior speci
men a me
mber of
a part

icular kind

class or group tax

on omic categ or

ya group distin

   guishable on

      one of a hier

arc hyof mutu

                ally X-clus

ɪᴠᴇ ᴄʟᴀꜱꜱᴇꜱ ɪᴨ ʟᴏɢɪᴄ

suggest ed to a

   void par

  ⴷᴅᴏ ᕽᴇꜱ ꜱᴏᴍᴇ

thing dist in guish

   able X-ting

           uishable as

   & so he E

      lewded D

         scription

          any kind of in

           scription

an ɢold word a tall

what every Canadian should know

(and probably does)

about language:

it's not what you think
not what you might suppose

not at all

that nor this
take the following
consider these examples
what about this
case that sentence
/these

English has lost most of its early vocabulary but it retains much of its
sound. Hence it is relatively easy for an English speaker to pronounce
German in a reasonable way. And vice-versa.

English has become an imperial language and infiltrated many
other languages, unstoppable glacier, inclined more to leavings than
receivings, moraines of its passage, though it has of course taken up
bits and pieces for centuries. Quite a lot actually. It, itself, was virtually

swamped by Latin, French, and Norse. English continues to swallow new words, can't help itself, pigs them down whole.

The nouns in Michif derive from French but all the verbs come from Cree.

The Norman conquerors, Norsemen by removal, brought with them their version of French, esteemed in law, the arts, government. It subsequently faced the cachet of Parisian French, which brought its own esteemed vocabulary, so that we now see traces of the Norman "w" and the Parisian "gu." Hence in English we have "warranty" and "guarantee," "reward" and "regard," "warden" and "guardian." So says the wag, gawking.

About 99% of words included in a large English dictionary come from some other language. About 62% of the most commonly used words come from Old English. No shit, said the learned scholar, fucking profound says the erudite grammarian.

Diglossia—to speak in two tongues. To speak with forked tongue.
When're yuh cumin' back? When will you return?
Hey, you kids should check out this. Pardon me, perhaps you children might examine this item.

when I think

of U I think of I

i mean

the I and the O

around which the other letters gather

in love & strife elemental

my father saying of them

the McKechney brothers that is

I can't tell them apart

unless I see them together

that I / that O

from which in thankful emulation

they take their lines

O I luv them   / I really do

I am thinking of the ancient I

that begat us that began as a twisted zag

in elbow & wrist & hand

the I that once was Yod

that reached out in arm & hand

                                        until the Greeks
                        got wind of it
                        got hold of it
                 once they laid hands on it
                    the jig was up they
                 gave it a darn good shaking they
                            gave it one hell of a talking to
                 & they straightened it
                                             out once & for all

by the time they were done
it was a mere nothing
couldn't help noting
it was a shadow of its former self
becoz they didn't care
one iota for yod showed
   no respect for its for
          king Y
not one jot did they care
for the wish bone they held once
their arms trembling with wonder
          the sounds whirring in their ears

                 & then when I 1 I
          ota shrank still more
          nearly vanished to a tick
          it became the smallest
          letter but 1 never known
          to shirk a chance for for
          mer glory mere vanity in search of
          distinction it developed
          a slanted view a flair
          which in insouciance it wears still in

but in time at last it lost

its nerve & dwind

led to a tiny

line un

der a dot

in its id

iot dot

age dim

in i shed

to a do

tted

lin

e

.

the
postmodern
journalist
dreams

gertrude stein reading e.e. cummings

(for GB at 70)

you don't know
what's what
or what
is more where
is where not
to mention where
why is why
& why
who is who how
when who is what
who is supposed to be when
why is what you want
more than why don't you

admit it then
admit it when
what is where
who is why then how
& where where is
why what when when is
what is when who is
where is why then

when where is who you are
wondering what is what
& who then is how where
why was now & there
is nowhere why is not

i kept a log : : :

went all the way the whole
hog from way back
i had the low down
realized the low goes
a long way had no wish
to take the high way
learnt how to photograph the cold
when to weigh the sun in a pan
why to be silent is mistaken
where to air divine is to know error

or of our ways also divine
ly to be wisht but i couldn't quite
put my tongue on it
not properly at least
not though i went into it
with my eyes wide open god knows
      i swam like a frog
      as bug-eyed
      id felt an itch
      had an id for it

mother tongue in which we write
      tongue i glued to
    the barrel in winter
raw and red when i pulled it off

to which we listen that hits
the spot to which she says
now don't give me away
don't give me any

of your lip don't go & get hyper
venti lating with me lately it's a matter of
        finding your hand
not losing your head
            some writing in it
your penchant for hyper

            bole lit ote too if it
            came to that holy smokes
            this smacks of the
            or y you know i don't
            know you one bit
                        but i do
                o idoidoidoido
            know a thing
            or two i under
            stand how well
            you go for N
            trances & of X
            its something i know
            some thing
            about IO & U
            owe me big

            its your own
            (or my) fault yd like id like
                to feel just once
            your tongue in my ear

your wet & slippery lips
the warm cursives of your moving
soft cruisings of your body

        all 26 parts of it
its hot & urgent appeals
every combination thereof
      for ever & ever
      word with out end
      ad in fin it um tum
      fee fie foe fum
      ble in lip id in all
      ease end lessly
      world with end
      everything gone
      end over end
      ever more
      over more
      & what is more
      there is

                no end to things
                she says
                a men to
                that that is

to hear her tell it

to hear her say
in a chalky sky
a chalky manner
here it is
this is it
this it is
there it is

neither there nor here
no where & no way
is this heresay
no nor is it heresy
for it is hers
            to say
we can count on
her say-so
so it is

hours to no
who's to say
it's pleurisy or
it's here to stay
who's to say
way to go

                                                    we say
                                                it's time to go
                                              here right here
                                            is what she meant
                                              to say to say

she meant what
is this what she saw
was this what he said
heretofore or before hand
counting out the digits
do you dig it some guy said
to the last decimal
of rechorded rhyme
to one in then

                                            & then there were nine
                                              nein sd the german
                                              s/he'll have nein of that
                                            was clear as a nun on that
                                              one can count on that
                                                on that we can be

ab so lutely certain
nine times out of ten   i mean honestly
anywhere you look   who can take this
whichever comes first   seriously i mean can you
which ever way you look at it   take it any more
you can take my word on it   or any where
when every one has already & always asked why can you
make anything
of it

ill is it

liaison
an illicit
sexual re
        latio
ns hip is it
sex is it
    ill is it
sex you all
wan der about
i sit ill al
ways sit i will
not annul an ill
its exual ann
its annual
it is nill
            the pro
        nun ciation an
        nunciation of
        an other wise ab
    sent con son ant so
        und at the end
            oft he first
            o ftwoc on
    secutive words the

second of which be

gins with a vow

el sound and foll

ows with

out pa

use

who is who

& which is
which
hand or not
hard to decide
between u & i
or is that me
who can give you
a few point
ers here &
now a bout
there & then

right about then then
right about now
things should get inter
esting things might get out
of hand if you don't
know what is what don't
know where you stand
if you don't grow a little
am, be dextrous, lee

it is neither
here nor there
but as for
that i said
that that that is

        there go i &
there i go again &
there there you say
why not have some more
why not have a little
fun a little fooling
    a round

                        ¿ with me

i do not want
to believe

it could happen like this
am not sure now it did happen

stepping out of the Prado
La Guernica on the wall
(was it there or do i only
¿ remember it there

the beasts bellowing the mangled
terror of eyes & arms

slam into a wall of light
the cicadas in trees
rewinding /an old film

a woman the woman who
¿ por favor senor
when you entered ¿ held
out her hand
grins now her friend offers
two stiff ears

death in the afternoon

aleph   *alpa*   *ox*
beth   *beta*   *house*

     the ox house

                   we speak & write in
                      a barn of bones
                the long & short of it
                      our long & short
                      bones of blood

the biologist goes acourting

"What small perversions of the
body make us sing?" — Robert Kroetsch,
The Hornbooks of Rita K

perhaps being stifled if not
detoxified if i'd or you'd
only listened to the talks you
might be de my
stified might if you had
testified paid attention been able
to hear the deoxyribonucleic acid then
and then there we have it
there it is—dna and

           then some

      letters—4 of them
which in miles of tangled correspondence
to & from & to & from & to & from to & from
the moon that langours so farly near

having written instructions
carried secret messages clear
to the proteins which in tumult squirm
which could be managed only if

the letters were to speak properly
                    words they found
           wise & winsome

if in speaking adenine it said it said
           guanine and then it said
cytosine and what is worse thymine
said how close you are   /to clementine
said why then don't you be mine
                    all in good thyme
oh sweet adenine thy mine is my mine

wrote letters that were not partic
ularly special in the steps they made
in the grand staircases where they swept
to the moon & back twice over
except when put in such a way

they climbed like Gatsby half way to the stars
           proved well nigh irresistible
                    in imperishable breath sang
sweet nothings in the language we all know
           forever & tirelessly runs between

     carried letters to the confused
                sent guidance to the lovelorn
     world which doubting speaks
           in terms it can or can
                not understand

behold it says for in this day
in the valley of Saskatchewan etc etc

skilled mediator it has made
an offer it is said it said
the protein could understand
and could not in any case refuse
        knew it would quicken
to a language they could not resist

you better believe

she was The Queen of The Hop
      & they had to
                hop to it
hope had little to do with it

she sent bees packing
      they were in her
    power for hours & hours
they were to scour the country
      for metaphors & magic (though there wasn't
much
         not in these parts there wasn't(

whats theirs is hers she announed
hers is hours she told them
she was from a land that rang veritably sang
    with milk & honey she told them
      time & again (it was tragic)
what they were and what they were not

to look for she was in charge
in fields & sloughs & streets
watched those who did not gild her
& she had identified knew for certain
just where & what the great lode was

this was after
she had sent her mate twanging to his death
trailing ribbons from a body she had ript open

when workers back from their earranty came back
covered with dirt and their faces wind-burnt
eyes bright and odd she could smell
irregular breath in their hosiery
there was a snag somewhere
there were /tickles in their ears
they had been getting & doing a little
steppin off & stompin in for
bidden fields something had gone haywire
she knew theyd gone off
the deep end you could depend on that
theyd gone bad
ly into debt into arrears
theyd got off on the wrong
foot they had been stepping out
of line losing time for some
rhyme or reason they could not keep
time the way they limped or walked
no sense of rhythm
they were one royal pain in the asss

she was put out and she was going
to put them
out of her tropical paradise out of their misery

          when she leaned

sweet eyes small beads   of sweat waxed

               just like that

   right out of the blue

                she got in

    the last word &

              dear god

her looks were killing

marshall broods over the creation

- print breaks up the tribe, he said, the man with the message
- print turns us inward, away from the tribe, into private thought, mullings, maulings of letters
- without letters, outside of literacy, people move like bats in the dark, take soundings, the world resounds with talk and chant and ululations, addresses the solidity of things, perhaps their solidarity, perhaps not
- it is a world of verbs and concrete reference, a world without print, a poetry some say—the oral world that is
- abstraction rises from alphabets we can take away and remove from the things of this world, the silent marks of idea and concept, ab-stracted, drawn away, drawn back, drawn, gone and gaunt
- the state of being verb scarcely exists before print has entered and come to dominate the experience of people: oh to be to be tobe tobe to
- without letters we turn to the typical, the colourful, the catching, the active, the combative, the vivid. also the outrageous, the flamboyant, the exaggerated, the stereotypical. how else to remember.
- the letter drains the colour from the world

- the letter silences the world. we silence words. he said. by writing down.
- the letter allows us to know new sounds, more colours. let loose
- an impatience to gain meaning means we do not read poetry aloud, fail to hear it really
- letters are streaks of black on white. for teachers they were white on black. to see the negative.
- the letter allows secret thoughts, unheard conversations with ourselves we sometimes call thinking, with others, those we never see, allows sedition, a fixed edition
- the letter "h" is a breathing sound
- so is the letter "a," a letting out, eh?
- print has brought freedom from old authorities
- print has brought control from new establishments
- newspapers are full of advertising and dependent on it. not the free but the kept press. it'll cost you. accost you too. our lives clipped & pressed, truly yclept—
- writers persist in straining language, staining it, straining it through, fall in love with the odd, the old, the new, the wonderful, the surprising, pleasing, displeasing, the inexpressible, the purloined, the unsaid, the often said, they assail the unsayable, indulge in dirty words, words we know and do not notice, smears and blotchings, wrenched letters, contorted fonts, dip in the font to be baptized, nonsense, doodle and babble, scribbles & cooings they put on quite a front an affront to good sense
- words whorled out of the world, whirled at it
- our mark for the interrogative <?> may well have come from the latin word "quaestio" when the first letter "q" was placed above the last letter "o" in a desire for speed in writing and clarity in reading. ¿quo vidas. oh to queue up for. as in printing: added to the tail and taken off the head, 0! the erotics of letters /that cue
- we send love letters to the world
- & who is there to see or read who to hear or listen

how can i

care about
what about

the man you script

the look you stole

in syn & hypo

thesis this is

"There really was no Greek theology in the sense that theology provides a coherent and profound explanation of the workings of both the cosmos and the human heart."*

the many cryptic letters
& hearts you have stript
have stopt /cold
you the unmoved mover

though the earth moves
what you have written in))or out of
love you with your pale O
　(such geo-)
-graphy so graphic not to men
tion -metry it is time
let me try let me say hi
time for me too me too
though i hadn't a glimmer
a new N-try a new B

ginning)im perial or me tric
why not why not go for me rit

why don't you when your hand moves
in fallacious curlicues & ma
jestic majuscules first let me
            slide down the hyp
o ten euse glide toward the acute art
        iculation if there is any
                use or cause
                    oughtened you
            if you are only going to be
                obtuse as all get out
insist on more than your musculature
your share of angles & degrees
if you are going to live by the law of the lever
turn to fiascoes of celestial tunings por poise in frisco bay
all you feel rustspots freckled inside your thin tin heart

in the mean time is it gout this seizure at the joints
        impecunious \peculiar
                        seeing as you are
you are i am we are
                    all over
the joint all over
        les billets doux
                    you & you

                ask then what
        about porn
                ography ? i don't
                think so i say i am
                so poor i don't

even have a por

no graph since

you up & gone

you gone away & left me

                all alone & blue

& i can't get over you

      not now i cant

      not now i met a met

      a physical you

*"science, history of." *Encyclopædia Britannica.*
Encyclopædia Britannica 2007 Ultimate Reference Suite.
Chicago: Encyclopædia Britannica, 2007.

come posit, or

(god for bid—

that we might
better comp
re: hend

com·pos·i·tor (km-pz-tr)
n.
One that sets writ ten ma terial in
to type; a type setter.

[Middle English compositur, *one who composes, settler of disputes,*
from An glo-No rman compo sitour, from Latin, *writer, co mpiler,*
from compn ere, composit-, *to put together*; see **component**.]

to clean! up

the text

proof·read (prfrd)
v. **proof·read** (-rd), **proof·read·ing, proof·reads**

v.tr.

To read (copy or proof) in order
to find errors and mark corrections.

v.intr.

To read copy or proof for pur
poses of error detection and correction

Acknowledgements

With thanks to the University of Alberta Press who have painstakingly seen this book into print, and especially to Alan Brownoff for his superb handling of a difficult text, and to Peter Midgley for his patient and exacting work as editor.

Several of these pieces have appeared or will have appeared elsewhere, usually in slightly different versions: "PREFACE" in Rampike; "Olito's suknaski" in *Andrew Suknaski: Essays on His Works*; "hyoid" and "lungs flapping" in *Jacket*; "as for me & my id," "at any and" in an Olive chapbook, "His Vernacular Prairie: Poems by Dennis Cooley"; "the postmodern journalist dreams" in *7i for GB: An anthology for George Bowering on the occasion of his 70th birthday*.